Copyright © 2018 Katherine Thorell
All rights reserved.

This book is dedicated to Kenneth, my devoted father.
The man who brought the Christmas dragon to life,
and who inspired me to dream.

# Jake the Dragon Saves Christmas

Written and Illustrated by
Katherine Thorell

# Jake the Dragon Saves Christmas

*Written and Illustrated by*
*Katherine Thorell*

Flying high in the sky
through sun and soft cloud
glides a young cheerful dragon
just exploring around.

Far down below he spotted a farm.
With cows, some chickens, and a great big red barn.

Inside the farm house a woman was making
oodles of Christmas goodies all waiting for baking.
Pies, cookies, and great big cakes too!
Nestled around some hazelnut stew.
For in a few hours her guests would be arriving.
Whether on foot, or horse, or others by driving.

The smells filled his nose and he wished he could be snuggled up peacefully beneath her big christmas tree.

Then all of a sudden, he heard a great shout
because in that instant all the lights had gone out!
He heard her say from across the room,

" Oh no! My party is certainly doomed! I can't bake my
goodies without the power and the party will start in
just over an hour. "

He made up his mind. He knew just what to do.
"Excuse me Miss, I think I can help you."
She turned her head to see who was there.
It was a young dragon with a white tuft of hair.

"Yes please come in. Now what can you do?"
"I can help bake if that's alright with you."

With that he sucked in a giant gulp of air
and let out a flame that broke her despair.

With a few puffs of his flame he had everything hot.
All the way down to the last buttery knot.
The soups were all bubbling, every cookie golden brown.
The turkey was juicy, and would taste great going down.

Then without warning an amazing delight.
Luminous and bright came on the lights.

And what a sight!

The table was full of more treats to chew.
Rolls, jams, and jellies, plus hot cocoa too.
Grean beans and potatoes it was a great feast.
From one course to the next there was so much to eat.

On a seperate table,
twice the size of your bed
were many desserts
from the bottom to the head.

Apple pies, gingerbread
and rolls filled with jelly.
All kinds of treats
to fill your empty belly.

Just as the last pie
was set down and placed,
noises from the yard
began to fill the empty space.
Friends and relatives
from far and near
had finally arrived
to join in the Christmas cheer.

After dinner was finished everyone joined in song.
Some songs were short and some songs were long,
but all were of Christmas full of joy and good cheer.
Hope for a blessed and happy new year.

When all was done and the guests had left Grandma and Jake settled down for a rest.

# Grandma's Gingersnap Recipe

Of all my families recipes, gingersnaps have always been my favorite. Their crunchy edges wrap around a soft middle. Sweet sugar nips at your tongue before being replaced by a warm sensation from the cloves, cinnamon, and ginger. The best part of all? It's a great recipe to do with a friend!

| | |
|---|---|
| 3/4 Cup | Shortening |
| 1 Cup | Brown sugar (light or dark) |
| 1/4 Cup | Mollasses |
| 1 | Egg |
| 2 1/4 Cups | Sifted flour |
| 2 tsp | Baking soda |
| 1/2 tsp | Salt |
| 1 Tbsp | Ginger |
| 1 tsp | Cinnamon |
| 1/2 tsp | Cloves |
| | Roughly 1 Cup of white sugar for rolling. |

Grab the nearest dragon and tell him to heat his belly to 375 degrees.

Have your little dragons grab a large mixing bowl. Cream together shortening, brown sugar, molasses, and an egg. Continue mixing until the mixture becomes light and fluffy.

In a seperate bowl, or empty dragons egg, start sifting together flour, baking soda, salt, ginger, cinnamon, and cloves. Save the white sugar for later. Incorporate dry ingredients into wet mixture. At this point, the dough should be smelling amazing!

To make things easier, you can place the mixture into the fridge for 10-20 minutes, but you don't have to. Use a small cookie scoop to form balls. Roll each ball in the white sugar to coat. Place them roughly 2 inches apart on a greased cookie sheet. Bake at 375 for 8-10 minutes. Gingersnaps made with dark brown sugar may take a few extra minutes to cook. If you like your cookies to snap, keep your cookies in the oven until you see them collapse.

After removing your cookies from the oven, let them cool on the pan for 1-2 minutes before placing them on a cooling rack.

Bakes 3 dozen cookies.

www.ingramcontent.com/pod-product-compliance
Lightning Source LLC
Chambersburg PA
CBHW042014090426
42811CB00015B/1646